I am an Express Bus

Copyright © 2024 by A Devi Thangamaniam.

All right reserved. No part of this publication may be reproduced, distributed, or transmitted in any form or by any means, including photocopying, recording, or other electronic or mechanical methods, without the prior written permission of the author, except in the case of brief quotations embodied in critical reviews and certain other non-commercial uses permitted by copyright law.

Information: MiLu Children's Educational Source

www.my-willing.com

ISBN: 979-8-88796-613-7

Vroom Vroom

I am an Express Bus

Welcome to everyone

I am from Lulia bus stand to Marian bus stand

I am looking forward to serving you.

I will reach on time.

Have a safe and happy trip.

Children aged 12 and under can travel fare-free.

Choose me

Get on and get off

Vroom Vroom

I am an Express Bus

Welcome to everyone

I am from Lulia bus stand to Marian bus stand

- Be at the bus stop five minutes before I arrive, please.
- Wait in a safe place, please.
- Stay away from the edge of the road, please.
- Stay away from me, please.

Now the time is morning at 7:00

I will reach at Marian bus stand morning at 8:10

Vroom Vroom

I am an Express Bus

Welcome to everyone

I am from Lulia bus stand to Marian bus stand

Line up in a single file, please.

Line up until the bus has stopped, please.

Line up until the bus has stopped and the door is fully open, please.

You did a great job.

It's a pleasure to you for cooperating with me.

Vroom Vroom
I am an Express Bus
Welcome to everyone

I am from Lulia bus stand to Marian bus stand

A little bit back, please.
Move a little bit back, please.
Further, move a little bit back, please.

Thank you so much for your understanding.
Your support allows passengers to get more space.

Now the time is morning at 7:05

Next bus stop is
Lulia street at Velvet Place

Vroom Vroom

I am an Express Bus

Welcome to everyone

I am from Lulia bus stand to Marian bus stand

Sit on your seat, please.
Sit on your seat properly, please.
Sit on your seat properly and straight, please.

I like the way of your sitting position.
Improve your motor skills and balance.

Now the time is morning at 7:10

Next bus stop is
Lulia street at Olive Drive

Vroom Vroom

I am an Express Bus

Welcome to everyone

I am from Lulia bus stand to Marian bus stand

Keep your pass, please.
Keep your bus pass, please.
Keep your bus pass yourself, please.

You are following the correct way.
This is a good way for using to travel.

Now the time is morning at 7:15

Next bus stop is
Lulia street at Mercury Place

Vroom Vroom

I am an Express Bus

Welcome to everyone

I am from Lulia bus stand to Marian bus stand

Need help, please.
A person need help, please.
A person with disability need help, please.

I appreciate your wonderful support.
Your support makes him have a comfortable journey.

Now the time is morning at 7:20

Next bus stop is
Lulia Street at Peach Orchard Place

Vroom Vroom

I am an Express Bus

Welcome to everyone

I am from Lulia bus stand to Marian bus stand

Speak in a soft voice, please.
Speak in a soft voice inside, please.
Speak in a soft voice inside the bus, please.

I am really happy that you speak in a calm voice.
You make a peaceful environment.

Now the time is morning at 7:25

Next bus stop is
Lulia Street at Lotus Garden

Vroom Vroom

I am an Express Bus

Welcome to everyone

I am from Lulia bus stand to Marian bus stand

Wait for the green light, please.
Wait for the traffic green light, please.
Wait for the traffic signal green light, please.

I really appreciate your patience.
It increases your self-control and discipline.

Now the time is morning at 7:30

Next bus stop is
Lulia street at Pigeons Drive

Vroom Vroom

I am an Express Bus

Welcome to everyone

I am from Lulia bus stand to Marian bus stand

Your arms and head inside, please.
Your arms and head inside the bus, please.
Keep your arms and head inside the bus, please.

I am so glad about your understanding.
This is a better way to prevent injuries.

Now the time is morning at 7:35

Next bus stop is
Lulia street at Poppy Avenue

Vroom Vroom
I am an Express Bus
Welcome to everyone

I am from Lulia bus stand to Marian bus stand

Wait, please.
Wait until the train is crossing, please.
Wait until the train is crossing the road, please.

I am very impressed by your waiting.
I wanted to thank you for continuing to listen.

Now the time is morning at 7:40

Next bus stop is
Lulia street at Thyme Square

Vroom Vroom

I am an Express Bus

Welcome to everyone

I am from Lulia bus stand to Marian bus stand

Stand away from the doors, please.
Stand away from the bus doors, please.
Stand away from all the bus doors, please.

I am really happy that you are staying safe.
This is more convenient for the passengers too.

Now the time is morning at 7:45

Next bus stop is
Lulia Street at Cherry Road

Vroom Vroom

I am an Express Bus

Welcome to everyone

I am from Lulia bus stand to Marian bus stand

Use the handrail, please.

Use the handrail when exiting, please.

Use the handrail when exiting the bus, please.

I am pleased about you for using the handrail.

It controls your body's support and balance.

Now the time is morning at 7:50

Next bus stop is Lulia street at Geese Circle

Vroom Vroom
I am an Express Bus
Welcome to everyone

I am from Lulia bus stand to Marian bus stand

Before crossing, stop, look, please.
Before crossing, stop, look both side, please.
Before crossing, stop, look both side and obey the traffic signal, please.

I am so proud of your acceptance.
It helps to pay attention to what is happening around you.

Now the time is morning at 7:55

Next bus stop is
Lulia street at Mallow Valley

Vroom Vroom

I am an Express Bus

Welcome to everyone

I am from Lulia bus stand to Marian bus stand

When crossing the road walk, please.
Always when crossing the road walk, please.
Always remember when crossing the road walk, please.

I am very pleased about your caring.
This is also a great way to protect from harm.

Now the time is morning at 8:00

Next bus stop is
Lulia street at Sunflower Farm

Vroom Vroom

I am an Express Bus

Welcome to everyone

I am from Lulia bus stand to Marian bus stand

Walk in front of me, please.
Walk away 10 steps from in front of me, please.
Walk away 10 big steps from in front of me, please.

Thank you for accepting this message.
A great way to protect ourselves.

Now the time is morning at 8:05

Next bus stop is Lulia street at Daisy Park

Vroom Vroom

I am an Express Bus

Welcome to everyone

I am from Lulia bus stand to Marian bus stand

The next bus stop is Marian bus stand.

This is my last stop.

Stay in your seat, please.

Stay in your seat until the bus has stopped, please.

Stay in your seat until the bus has completely stopped, please.

I am so glad you enjoyed and have a safe trip.

You did a great job and I am very proud of you.

Now I am at Marian bus stand

Now the time is at morning 8:10

Thank you for choosing me.
I admire the way you engaged in this trip.

See you next time
Have a nice day
Bye Bye

www.ingramcontent.com/pod-product-compliance
Lightning Source LLC
LaVergne TN
LVHW070541070526
838199LV00076B/6820